Power Points 4 Living

Practical Applications for a Successful Life

TISHA REID

POWER POINTS 4 LIVING:
PRACTICAL APPLICATIONS FOR A SUCCESSFUL LIFE
Copyright © 2021 Tisha Reid

All rights reserved. No part of this book may be reproduced or transmitted in any form or by any means, electronic or mechanical, including photocopying, without written permission from the publisher.

Power Points 4 Living, L.L.C.
www.powerpoints4living.com
info@powerpoints4living.com

Scripture quotations marked (KJV) are taken from the KING JAMES VERSION (KJV): KING JAMES VERSION, public domain.

Scripture quotations marked (NLT) are taken from the Holy Bible, New Living Translation, copyright ©1996, 2004, 2015 by Tyndale House Foundation. Used by permission of Tyndale House Publishers, Inc., Carol Stream, Illinois 60188. All rights reserved.

Scripture quotations marked (NKJV) are taken from the New King James Version®. Copyright © 1982 by Thomas Nelson. Used by permission. All rights reserved.

Scripture quotations marked (NIV) are taken from the Holy Bible, New International Version®, NIV®. Copyright © 1973, 1978, 1984, 2011 by Biblica, Inc.™ Used by permission of Zondervan. All rights reserved worldwide. www.zondervan.com The "NIV" and "New International Version" are trademarks registered in the United States Patent and Trademark Office by Biblica, Inc.™

Scripture quotations marked (NET) are taken from the NET Bible® http://netbible.com copyright ©1996, 2019 used with permission from Biblical Studies Press, L.L.C. All rights reserved.

Scripture quotations marked (NASB) are taken from the (NASB®) New American Standard Bible®, Copyright © 1960, 1971, 1977, 1995, 2020 by The Lockman Foundation. Used by permission. All rights reserved. www.lockman.org

Scripture quotations marked (NLT) are taken from the Holy Bible, New Living Translation, copyright ©1996, 2004, 2015 by Tyndale House Foundation. Used by permission of Tyndale House Publishers, a Division of Tyndale House Ministries, Carol Stream, Illinois 60188. All rights reserved.

Prepared for Publication by:
Rev/12 Publishing
www.rev12publishing.com

Cover Image: Photographed by Daryl W. Arnold
Chapter Images: Photographed and Designed by Tisha Reid
Chapter Reflection Images: pngtree.com; https://consciouslivingmagazine.com.au/sounding-calm/female-1299085_1280/; https://www.dreamstime.com/royalty-free-stock-images-woman-hands-prayer-image29670049

Library of Congress Cataloging-in-Publication Data is available upon request.
ISBN: 9780578873572

Printed in the United States of America
Independently Published

DEDICATION

This book is dedicated to my husband – my life partner, Rodric K. Reid, for supporting the ministry work that God has given me. I also dedicate this book to our three gifted children: Jasmin, Tiffani, and Jessica Reid. I love you all to life.

CONTENTS

Acknowledgments ix

Foreword x

Introduction xiii

Chapter 1: Live 3

    LIVE One Breath at a Time 6

    Living is Resting 9

    LIVE With Your Anthem Song 11

    LIVE Intentionally 12

    Choose to LIVE 15

    LIVE & G.R.O.W. 18

    Powerful Reflection & Application 22

Chapter 2: Pray 33

    Prayer is Communication 34

    Purpose of Prayer: Commune with God 38

    Purpose of Prayer: Increase our Faith 41

    Prayer is a Powerful Weapon 43

    Lord Teach us to Pray 44

    Powerful Reflection & Application 47

Chapter 3: Forgive 57

    Forgive for the Health of It 58

    What is Forgiveness? 60

    Forgive Yourself 63

Forgiveness is a Process	66
How Many Times Do We Forgive?	70
Powerful Reflection & Application	74
Summary	81
Current Resources	83
About the Author	85

ACKNOWLEDGMENTS

I must first thank God for trusting me with this project and for His guidance. I have to thank our oldest daughter, Jasmin Reid, for providing her insightful feedback and support. Rachelle Clark, thank you for your friendship and for listening to me talk about this project for years.

This book would not have been able to come to life without Uplift Ministries, Inc., and the Women's Empowerment Prayer Team: Rachelle Clark, Barbara Ervin, Rolunda Fears, Anna Molton, Crystal Payne, Beverly Watkins, and Rev. Kendah Ward. Thank you, women of God, for your intercessory work in the conferences and this book.

Finally, I really would not have been able to move forward with this project without the years of support and love from my husband, Rodric K. Reid. You believed in me when I didn't believe in myself. Thank you for supporting my dreams by reading my book drafts, providing invaluable wisdom, prayers, and encouragement.

"I Love you, and there is nothing you can do about it."

FOREWORD

For more than 30 years, I have been devoted to the ministry of uplifting people from all walks of life to reaching self-sufficiency through a relationship with God. Through this wonderfully burdensome blessing that God has placed upon my life, I have come to realization of this one thing ... life is hard! Regardless of where you come from, what you do or do not have, or your level of education, each day has the potential to journey you through an emotional tornado of events that at times, if we be honest, makes us entertain the notion to just give up.

On November 25, 1980, famed boxers Sugar Ray Leonard and Roberto Durán would face off for the second time in the ring in pursuit of the World Boxing Council (WBC) Welterweight Championship of the world. Both men had trained for months and were in phenomenal condition. As they took the ring with great expectation of victory, they began to play out before the entire world their gifts. As the fight progressed, it became evident that Durán was running out of answers to overcome his opponent who seemed to attack him from every direction. By the end of the 7th round, you could see the spirit of victory vanish from his eyes. Then it happened... in the 8th round, Durán turned his back to the fight and said: "No más" ("No more" in Spanish). He was so badly beaten that he gave up the fight. He voluntarily relinquished his opportunity for victory. After all, there were still seven more rounds to go. He gave up the possibility that things could turn in his favor. He lost hope in what could be. How many times have you been so overwhelmed by life that you felt like turning your back on the fight and saying "No más?"

Power Points 4 Living: Practical Applications for a Successful Life, is a wonderful guide grounded in simple biblical principles that render answers that will help you stay in the fight and ultimately find victory. Tisha Reid so plainly places before you real-life situations and offers you sound practical pathways to overcome those issues. She calls you to recognize the anatomy of life's trials beginning with taking a good look at where you are and where you want to be.

Then, she reminds you of who you truly are — "a chosen generation, a royal priesthood, a holy nation, a peculiar people that you should show forth the praises of him who has called you out of darkness into his marvelous light." (1 Peter 2:9 KJV)

Dr. Myles Monroe once said, "Your destiny is chosen by God, but its fulfilment is decided by you." Tisha Reid offers a clarion call for all to make a cognitive decision to walk in their divine destiny. Destiny is your soul's call to greatness. Destiny serves as a road map not only to your hopes and dreams but also to the exact place that God has ordained you to be from the beginning of time. When one begins to walk in their destiny, they are truly carrying out the assignment that God has for them. But walking in the assignment of God does not exempt any of us from experiencing the trials and tribulations that Jesus promised that this world would bring.

This gets to the heart of this book. *Power Points 4 Living: Practical Applications for a Successful Life* will give you step-by-step instructive biblical principles to effective living. Tisha uses her personal life trials and shows how prayer, forgiveness, intentional living, trueness of self, and a devotion to God helped her become the strong and overcoming woman of God she is today. She offers valuable life lessons to guide you from existing to destiny living. This book will turn your "No más," to "Yeah más."

Rodric K. Reid
Senior Pastor
Mt. Vernon Avenue AME Church
Columbus, OH

INTRODUCTION

Power Points for Living: Practical Applications for a Successful Life is meant to be an easy read. It is a conversation I'm having with you in hopes that you will have a deeper conversation with yourself and God.

Why did I write this book? It originated from me listening to God, then being obedient to what I heard. God told me to cover these topics in a women's conference and then write a supplemental book. If you did not attend any of the conferences, that is okay. I believe this book will still be a blessing to you. Additionally, *Power Points 4 Living: Practical Applications for a Successful Life* is not only for individual empowerment, but it can be used in group settings (book clubs, women's ministry, other church ministries, or as a family activity).

My prayer is that you will not only read this book in its entirety with an open heart but also dig deep, meditate over the powerful reflection questions, and be transparent with yourself. I pray something resonates with you. I pray that it empowers you to implement new activities and thought processes **that benefit you**, as well as your relationship with others and God.

I sincerely thank you for supporting this ministry work, and I thank God for moving in your life.

You have the power within to live, love, experience forgiveness, freedom, and be successful.

Live on Purpose!

Live Abundantly

ZŌĒ (dzo-ay')

of the absolute fulness of life, both essential and ethical, which belongs to God, and through him both to the hypostatic "logos" and to Christ in whom the "logos" put on human nature

---

Chapter 1

Live

I am fearfully and wonderfully made on purpose for a purpose.

The first Power Point for Living is to LIVE.

LIVE. What does that mean to you? Does it simply mean you are alive? Does it mean that you do any and everything you are big and bad enough to do? You know the saying, Y.O.L.O. — "You Only Live Once so you better enjoy it any way you can." Take a moment and reflect. What does "LIVE" mean for me? Are you really living or just existing?

I need you to understand that there is a difference between living and existing. Many of us have been going through life just existing. Existing can be defined as just the state of being. Some of us are just in a state of waking up in the morning, eating, rushing off to work, coming back home, cooking dinner, doing chores around the house, paying bills, getting on social media, watching our favorite television show, and going to bed. We wake up the next day and repeat. We are just existing. Let me give you another example. This book that you are reading now existed in my mind. Until I purposed to move beyond thinking and go through the process of writing and publishing, it didn't become a living manuscript. You, too, may have a piece of paper that's just existing, but until you do something with it no one will ever see your manuscript come to life. To live is to be FULL of life. It is the continuation of existing. When God formed man he just existed, but when God breathed the breath of life into him, man became a living soul (Genesis 2:7). When man became a living soul, he walked in his purpose. He loved and took ownership over what had been given to him. God wants us to recall and reclaim our Genesis; our beginning and our purpose — and take ownership of it. He wants us to live life to the fullest and do good things. God wants our life to be full of energy, joy, and peace.

> *For we are God's masterpiece. He has created us anew in Christ Jesus, so we can do the good things he planned for us long ago. (Ephesians 2:10 NLT)*

God is saying, "I want you to live! There is more to life than just existing, and I want you to experience all that I have for you."

Even in times of crisis or pandemics, you can still do more than exist. You were created on purpose for a purpose. You may not know what your purpose is, and your purpose may change over time, but everyone has *purpose* placed *inside* of them by God.

I do not believe that there is another Tisha. There is no one else like me. I would dare say that there is no one else like you either. We are unique. There is only one you. We are special with all of our strengths and flaws. I believe the Word of God that tells us that we are fearfully and wonderfully made. God took His time in making us. We are His artwork — His masterpieces. We are beautifully and strategically made on purpose for a purpose. You are not an accident. I am not an accident. God doesn't create mistakes. He creates original masterpieces world-wide. It doesn't matter where you are in this life today. No matter what chapter your autobiography is in, you are a unique masterpiece created in love. Believe it and say this out loud:

"I will praise You, for I am fearfully and wonderfully made;"
(Psalm 139:14 NKJV)

Therefore, please understand that you and I are not mistakes. God did not create us to live in misery but to live abundantly. Jesus said in his Word:

"I came that you might have life and life more abundantly."
(John 10:10)

The word life here in Greek is "Zoe" (ZOH-ee). Zoe is the highest and best type of life. It is a life devoted to God in fellowship with Christ. A life focused on the promises; a life that trusts God with our physical and spiritual needs. God wants us to have this "Zoe." He wants us to experience life with Him that produces love, joy, peace, patience, kindness, goodness, faithfulness, gentleness, and self-control. God wants us to have a heaven-on-earth life, a *Zoe* life that is full of spiritual blessings that ultimately leads to eternal life with Him. Jesus did not sacrifice His life for us to just exist. Therefore, we are not to live life haphazardly but live life more abundantly in all of its fullness.

There may be someone reading this that can't perceive this type of Zoe life. You may be feeling helpless and hopeless. You need to know that this life is available even to you. Yes, you; the oppressed you, the abused you, the broken you. God wants to give you a life full of blessings — a life that is operating in the overflow — a life that is more than just existing.

I want you to stop reading right now and take a moment to breathe. Are you ready?

Now, take your breath back. Right now — take a deep breath. Inhale for about five seconds and breathe out (exhale) for seven seconds. Go ahead and do it; breathe in and breathe out. Just relax... isn't that good? Now, do it again. Take your breath back. Just breathe in... and breathe out. If you're breathing, you're moving. If you're moving, you're living. BREATHE. That's life. Simple.

LIVE ONE BREATH AT A TIME

The question some may ask is, "How can I live life to the fullest when all hell is going on all around me?" Answer: One breath at a time. One step at a time. One prayer at a time. Seek God and His resources that He's provided to strategically put out the fires surrounding you. For example, if you have more bills than money, don't ignore the bill collector's mail or phone calls. Instead, call on God and the companies you owe. Try to make payment arrangements with them, or go see a financial counselor. Consider consolidating your bills; one breath... one step at a time. Review your monthly spending and cut out non-essentials. If we are in a global crisis, take advantage of the resources provided by the government. Research them and if they are good and you qualify, complete your application to get the needed help.

If you want to stop smoking, pray and ask God for deliverance and utilize His resources. Contact the 1-800-Quit Now line or other tobacco cessation resources. If you are vaping or dabbing, text DITCHJUUL to 88709 and take it one breath at a time, one step at a time.

Maybe your loved one died, and you are wondering what your life is worth. Your life has value. Both your loved one and God would want you to keep moving, move past existing, and live. So, BREATHE. Inhale the love of Christ, and exhale the negativity of your reality. Take it one breath and one step at a time. Discover your new purpose. Try some new, wholesome things, or start a new business. Nurture existing relationships. These are some ways you can get your breath back. Get rid of the clutter in your life. Clean out the house, garage, or basement, and redecorate. Cancel some subscriptions you really don't need. Get rid of cable with all of those channels you never watch and just have a streaming service. Take it one step at a time, one breath at a time.

Maybe none of those are your issues, but whatever your issues are, don't let them overcome you. Pray and ask God to help you. In some cases, God will deliver you immediately. Others, He may require you to do something or use His resources in an act of obedience. Then, there are some things we cannot do anything about. Some like to call those, "thorny issues." These are issues that just remain like the Apostle Paul's in the Bible. And, just like Paul, we must also hold on to God's Word believing God will keep us and strengthen us.

> *"...My grace is sufficient for you, for My strength is made perfect in weakness." (2 Corinthians 12:9 NKJV)*

Hold on. Don't give in or give up. Breathe. Trust that you are only walking THROUGH the valley of the shadow of death. Trust that God is with you and will take you through to the other side and goodness and mercy will follow you (Psalm 23). Breathe through it.

No matter what your issues are, take a long look in the mirror, then take a deep breath, smile, and just love you. Love the skin you're in with all its scars (testimonies) and imperfections. Love you because God loves you. Love you because you were fearfully and wonderfully made! You are not your problems. You are not your issues.

Take a breath.

Loving you includes loving your character enough not to "act a fool." In dealing with an immediate confrontation, take a breath and think before you speak. You do not have to say everything you're thinking or go off on someone to prove a point. In the scripture, James 1:19 challenges us to be quick to listen, slow to speak, and slow to become angry. This even applies to how you provide immediate feedback to your children and loved ones. Take a breath and think before you speak. Speak firm but with love. Take each day and each issue one breath and one step at a time. Your life is worth every breath.

LIVING IS RESTING

Living one breath at a time also means you must take time for yourself to rest and recharge. Even God rested on the seventh day. He rested and reflected. Therefore, we need to do the same. We need to rest, reflect, and think about good things.

There are benefits to resting. Rest is good for your brain, spirit, and physical health. Rest includes setting boundaries for home and work. When you're home, try setting aside at least one hour just for you, also known as "me time." Do something that brings you peace or joy and takes your mind off the problems and mundane work. It could be a quiet time in meditation and prayer, sitting outside on your patio, taking a walk, gardening, taking a hot bath, or simply dancing like no one is watching.

Rest is vital to our body and mind. Therefore, let's make rest a priority. We all understand that work is important, but *rest is necessary*. Don't make the mistake of taking work home and letting it consume you, robbing you of your rest, family time, and sanity. Set your boundaries. When you're at work, stop working at lunch. Lunch is your rest time. Even if you work from home, you still need to set boundaries and take breaks. It is important that whether you're in the field or at home working you take your breaks and lunches. If you're working from home, get away from the computer, go outside and breathe some fresh air on your break. During your workday, incorporate mindfulness by focusing on one object (plant, fish, picture…) and clear your mind. Just relax your brain and give it a break. Take a 15-minute "cat nap" or power nap. Now, when you have deadlines that is understandable. However, some of us are working over lunch or taking work home out of habit, or trying to make an impression at the cost of our sanity, family, and necessary rest time. Use your breaks and lunches to steal away, get quiet, rest, and reflect so you can hear from God and be recharged.

According to the National Heart, Lung, and Blood Institute, sleep can improve your problem-solving skills, heal and repair your heart and blood vessels, decrease your chances of mood swings, Alzheimer's, obesity, and other chronic diseases. Rest improves our social and emotional intelligence. Rest is necessary for our ability to live abundantly one breath at a time.

We need our sleep. I implore you to choose sleep over worrying. The Bible says to "Be anxious for nothing... " (Philippians 4:6-7).

Go to bed. Trust God. Worrying about it will not change it. Instead, get your rest so your mind can refocus, recharge, and experience God's peace.

Think about it this way. If you don't take moments to rest and take time for yourself, you will not be any good to anyone else. Know this... even Superwoman or Superman needed a break. Better yet, remember God "rested" on the seventh day.

You might also consider incorporating walking into your daily life. Walking is one of the best mental health breaks everyone needs. You know the saying, "I'm going out to clear my head." Well, there is some science behind that statement. It works! Take a walk... one step at a time and one prayer at a time, breathing one breath at a time. It will change your life. It will change how you interact with people around you and how you respond to the ugly colors of this world. Take a breath and put up your umbrella as you go through the storms of life. Thank God for the rain and know that it will not last forever, understanding that the rainbow of promise comes afterward. Don't let this world choke the life out of you. Rest, reflect, and recharge.

LIVE WITH YOUR ANTHEM SONG

What else can you do when all hell is showing its ugly colors? Answer: Have an anthem song. One suggestion I received at a leadership conference was to have your own anthem song. What would be your anthem? Maybe it could be, "I Will Survive" by Gloria Gaynor, "Happy" by Pharrell, "Rise" by Andra Day, or maybe your anthem song is, "Roar" by Katy Perry. Maybe it is the Gospel song that records, "All things are working for my good, He's intentional" by Travis Greene. It could be Aretha Franklin's song, "RESPECT" because you want people to respect you, and you are going to R. E. S. P. E. C. T. them. Better yet, your anthem could be that silly song from back in the day, "Don't Worry Be Happy," or, the "Double Dutch Bus." The anthem can be a country, rap, or rock song. It is whatever can get you going in the morning and put a smile on your face. Again, I ask you... what's your anthem song? Let it be your alarm clock in the morning so that when you wake up, you can feel like, "ahhh... alright — I can do this."

Playing your anthem song in the morning can make your day brighter. Play it and start your day in the positive before the negative has a chance to creep in. Start in the positive before someone has a chance to get on the back of your last nerve. Then at least you have started out on the "good foot" or praising God. If someone comes and disturbs that state of happiness with their demands, negative attitudes, or drama, you can download your anthem song... and say within yourself, "I <u>Will Rise</u> above you. I'm going to respect you even though you don't respect me."

Because (singing)...

"I'm happy... Clap along if you feel like happiness is the truth. Because I'm happy... Clap along if you know what happiness is to

you. Because I'm happy... Clap along if you feel like that's what you wanna do...."

Overall, be positive in the midst of the negative surroundings. Some people are waiting and hoping to see you fail, "act a fool," or just give up. Don't satisfy them or give them a reason to be right. Instead, be positive, or as my mother used to say, "Never let them see you sweat." Speak positive affirmations over your life or your situation and sing your anthem song daily.

LIVE INTENTIONALLY

God wants us to live life and life more abundantly. To do this, we need to be intentional about how we're living. Please understand that living an abundant life does not exempt us from problems. The Bible tells us that we will have many trials and sorrows but to be of good cheer because Jesus has overcome the world (John 16:33). Even if we have played our anthem song and prayed, the problem may still be there. The question is, how are you dealing with the problem? We can ignore some things but others we cannot. There could be something ugly that comes across your desk or email at work. How are you going to react to that "nasty gram?" First, you need to "fix your face." Then, be intentional about pulling the positive out of it (no matter how small it may be) and write a professional response that does not jeopardize your position or your integrity. Focus on the dim light in the darkness. Intentionally take the negative things and turn them into positives. Remember to breathe in and breathe out. Seek out God's resources that He has placed around us. Some of those resources may include discounted counseling services from a Pastor, free employer mental health resources, clinics, financial counselors, shelters, housing assistance, free legal services, or even government assistance.

Not only should we be intentional in how we handle problems, but we also need to be intentional about our spiritual, mental, and physical health. You can work on your physical health by making a healthcare appointment, eating healthier, and incorporating some form of exercise (walking, yoga, strength training) at least three times a week. You can also take a walk in your neighborhood, take up bike riding, or dance to a video in between zoom meetings. Go outside and put your feet in the grass and breathe. At night, go out and gaze at the stars and think about good things. Decide to cut out sugar and eat healthier meals and snacks. Don't even buy junk food. Make an effort to stop watching violent, negative-filled television shows. Instead, read a book, work on your vision plan, or play games with the family. Enjoy the simple things in life that we don't think about anymore. You can "pay it forward" and do something kind for someone.

Intentionally work on your marriage. Place love notes in your spouse's work bag or on the bathroom mirror. Plan a special night with your spouse... just because. Get up early to have 15 minutes of conversation with them or cook them something to eat. Be a blessing to your spouse. Be intentional with your children too. It doesn't matter how old they are. Write a letter to your children expressing your love and proud moments. Be intentional in your finances. Make a budget and stick to it.

Last, but most importantly, intentionally put God on your daily calendar. Make an appointment with God and keep it. Set an alarm just for Him. Set up some new goals or habits that are beneficial to your whole being and help you not just to exist, but live the abundant life. Why is this necessary? Because the Bible tells us that life is more than food and a body is more than clothing. In other words, ... life is more than just existing paycheck to paycheck. Since life is more than these things, understand that it's not worth working yourself to death (sometimes literally) to the point that you can't enjoy life. God wants us to truly live. Again, our living …. our life…. is more than food and the body. It is more than raiment …. more than clothing. Life is more than going to work, worrying about bills, and repeating the "existing train" daily. It is more than the corner office, title, BMW, house, Versace, nails, and social media status. Life is so much more than the "things." Remember these words and keep them somewhere visible:

Seek first the kingdom of God and His righteousness and then all of these other things will be added unto you. (Matthew 6:33)

Willfully seek God and the things of God. Seek peace, joy, love, His communion, and to be in right standing with God. Seeking God will result in you living an abundant life, and will also provide you with all of those other "things."

You are important to God. He loves you so much. If no one else has told you that God loves you, I'm telling you... **God loves _you_**. I may not know you, but I love you with the love of God. I want you to know that all things are possible with Him and through Him. So, if you want to live this life intentionally in abundance, you must first understand that our living; our success is with God. If you have never believed in God or accepted Him as your Lord and Savior, you can do that right now. The Bible tells us in John 3:16 that "God so loved the world that He gave His only son that whosoever believes in Him shall not die, but have eternal life." God wants you to live forever! Remember, Jesus came so you can live that abundant life on earth and with Him. It's about the spiritual blessings of God. He wants to bless you with peace, joy, and so much more. He wants to spend an eternity with you.

If you have not really included God to be a part of your everyday life, but you want him to be, invite Him for the first time, or back again into your life and your heart. Be intentional about truly *LIVING* and receive God's abundant life by praying this prayer with me:

Dear God, thank You for loving me so much. Forgive me for the things I've done, thought, or said that were not pleasing in Your sight. Forgive me for all of my wrongdoings. I am so sorry. I want You to be my God — my Lord. I believe in You. I accept Your Son, Jesus, as my Lord and Savior, and I believe that You raised Him from the dead. Come into my heart. Be my God. I want to live life and life more abundantly with You. In Jesus's name. Amen.

CHOOSE TO LIVE

If you prayed that prayer, that is the first step to living life in abundance. Congratulations! We have to choose to live spiritually and physically. The Bible says I shall live and not die (Psalms 118:17). You have to choose to live. You have to choose to be that person and get away from the negativity and negative thinking people. You might be that Superwoman or Superman but remember "super" comes from God. You were not created to be super busy, but to be "super" connected and filled with His power, His strength, and His will. God is our power source. God endows you with the power to keep on going. He gives you that power to keep on moving. Choose to take time for yourself. Choose not to give up but to stand up.

Gospel artist Donnie McClurkin sings …. *"After you've done all you can, you just stand."* And God tells us in Ephesians chapter six, to put on the whole armor of God and stand. You might have lost a loved one, had an abortion, been sexually or physically abused, filed for bankruptcy, was served an eviction notice, furloughed on your job, been incarcerated, or just lonely. Choose not to wallow in those issues and rise up, calling on God for direction. Acknowledge God in ALL of your ways, and He will direct your paths (Proverbs 3:5-6). His directions may include using some of God's resources, like a physician or therapist. We may need those experts ordained by God to address any hormonal imbalances, assist us with nutrition intake that can boost our moods, or other techniques to assist with addictions or post-traumatic stress. Choose to trust God with it all. Believe me when I say this: "It is NOT the end of the world." It may seem like it, but it is not. You shall live! You will beat this. You shall overcome — whatever! So... choose to LIVE.

Can I be honest with you? There was a time when I just wanted to give up. Too many things hit me all at once, but I said to myself, "Oh no, I shall live and NOT die to proclaim the works of the Lord!" I made a decision to LIVE. I made a decision to try this abundant life Jesus was talking about.

Please be aware that even after you choose to physically live... or choose to stop *existing* and live.... you may still have feelings that want to keep you down and bound up. You must push through the feelings and intentionally make a decision and choose to live. Choose to live life and live life to its fullest. You have to go beyond the circumstances and rise above the pain, the hurt, the disappointment, or the infidelity. Rise above the loneliness, the sickness, the abuse, and pick yourself up.

CHOOSE TO LIVE. You are not your circumstances. Don't let your circumstances, mistakes, or feelings of shame redefine you. There is purpose in you, for you are "fearfully and wonderfully made" on purpose for a purpose! Don't focus on your age, nor the negative situation, problem, or people. When I was surrounded by negativity and problems, I also intentionally chose to shift my focus. The problem was still there, but I sought God and strategically began thinking about all those things that are good, true, noble, just, lovely, and of a good report. I refused to have pity parties, be around negative people, or let problems control me or my attitude. Two years ago, I placed on my bathroom mirror a card from the American Heart Association that only has hearts on the outside with these words:

"I Choose to Live."

That card is still there. It is a daily reminder that I will intentionally eat healthier, get moving, take time for myself, focus on the positive, and stop existing. It is my reminder that I am a real woman of change, and with God, all things are possible. It is a reminder that God loves me and created me to LIVE life to the fullest. It reminds me that no matter what, I choose to LIVE! How about you? Say it out loud:

> I CHOOSE TO LIVE. I AM DONE EXISTING.
> I SHALL LIVE AND NOT DIE
> TO DECLARE THE WORKS OF THE LORD!
> I CHOOSE TO LIVE!

You see, all things are possible with God and through Him. God wants you to ***LIVE*** life. He wants you to have that "Zoe" life. He wants to bless you with peace, joy, all those "things" and so much more. God wants to spend eternity with you because he loves you so much. Once you choose to live deliberately, apply the acronym G.R.O.W. in your daily living. This will be a reminder of how to live that abundant life.

LIVE & G.R.O.W.

<u>G</u> is for Greet the Giver of Life. Greet God every day. Let Him be the first one you speak to when you get up in the morning. Literally, open up your mouth and greet him with gratitude. Maybe you greet Him with something like, "Good morning, God! Thank You for letting me wake up this morning. Even though I don't want to face what I have to face… if You are with me, it will be alright;" or, "Good Morning God. Thank you for the breath in my body." Before you roll over and pick up your cell phone to check email, Facebook, Snapchat, Instagram, TikTok, or Pinterest, greet God. Before you roll over and pick up a cigarette or anything else, lay there — be still and just tell God, "Good morning." Greet the Giver of Life first and then rise.

<u>R</u> is for Rise. Rise up out of the pit of depression. We are not talking about clinical depression for that is a medical real issue. We are talking about when you are just having your pity party. When you feel like you've been attacked in almost every area of your life: home, finances, relationships, career, children, and/or health. If you have ever had this experience and you feel like the weight of the world is on your shoulders holding you down, let praise be your elevator. Psalm 42:11 tells us to put our hope in God and have a "yet praise."

> *Why art thou cast down, O my soul? and why art thou disquieted within me?* **hope thou in God**: *for I shall* **yet praise him**, *who is the health of my countenance, and my God. (KJV)*

For example, I may not have a job, *YET* I will praise you for opening doors in my favor and blessing me with fruitful employment. I may have some discord in my relationships, *YET* I will praise you for peace that passes all understanding and mending what is broken. Can you hope in God — no matter what it looks like? Do you have a *YET* praise?!

You cannot stay down, but you have to pull on the strength you have, open your mouth with a *YET* praise, and rise up. Rise up out of the mess. Rise up out of mediocrity. Rise up out of fear. Rise up out of feelings of failure and despair. Rise up, putting your hope in God and vocalizing your "yet praise." Rise up by thanking God in the midst of your situation. As hard as it may be, thank God. Thank Him for being God. Thank Him for keeping you. Thank Him in advance for what He's about to do. Worship Him. Then start working on being the change that you want to see.

Be intentional about your comeback and living an abundant life. Rise up with your anthem song. Rise up to *Roar* or *Great is Thy Faithfulness*... morning by morning, new mercies I see. Rise up to your anthem song! Get in the elevator of love, power, and of a sound mind, and rise from below ground to higher ground with God.

O is for Own it. Sometimes we like to blame a whole lot of people as the reason why things aren't going right in our lives. However, the truth of the matter is that some of the stuff we cause ourselves. So, whatever it is, even if you didn't cause it, you still "own" the situation that you're in. Don't deny it. For example, if the doctor and test results said you have an ailment... okay, that's what they said. Now your prayer could be ...."alright, it's me and You, Lord... come and tell me where I need to go and what I need to do. Let's get the best doctors and the best regiment of whatever needs to be done. I trust You, Lord, to take care of me and this _____, for You are Jehovah Rapha, the God who heals me."

Another example is if you spend all of your money on shopping, eating out every day, $50+nails and daily Starbucks, don't blame your job because they don't "pay you enough" or your children because you have to feed them. Be a good steward — a good manager over everything God has given you. Own the fact that you are spending too much unnecessarily, put yourself on a budget, and give yourself a raise.

Own It. Own whatever "it" is, and take responsibility. Taking responsibility brings peace of mind when you've done right.

<u>**W**</u> is for Walk. Walk in the physical and spiritual blessings of God. Walk, no matter what. As we mentioned earlier, science has proven that walking is good for Alzheimer's, your mental health (especially anxiety and depression), your cardiovascular, and endocrine systems. Spiritually, it also demonstrates one's resilience and faith as one gets up regardless of how many times they get knocked down.

I was in an accident and suffered from a traumatic brain injury. This injury was life changing. One of the immediate results was my inability to walk. Barely being able to move my feet, it would take forever to go from my bed to my bedroom door. I was off-balance and could only take little bitty steps at a time. I thought this was going to be the new me. Concerned, I talked to my neurologist about it and other problems I had. His answer was, "Just keep walking."

He told me that even though I was in pain, off balanced, and couldn't see myself getting better and walking like I used to, I just needed to trust him. He said, "If you just kept walking, your brain would tell your body to heal itself!" So, I'm telling you: "Whatever little steps you can take by faith, rise up, own it, and walk!" Even if you're still walking in mess, even if the ground is still a little bit dirty, you just keep on walking. Through the pain and frustration, you just keep walking. Even when you can't see it getting any better, you just keep walking. Walk until you get a bigger pep in your step. Walk until you get through the valley. You keep walking until that walk becomes a jog. You keep walking until one day you are running, and maybe the next you are soaring like an eagle. You just keep on walking.

    Walk in confidence with God. Sometimes all you can take are those little bitty steps to get there, and that's okay. Take it one step and one breath at a time. Don't you stop. Don't you quit. Don't you give in. You just keep walking. In other words, you just keep moving no matter what. You do all that you can, and then when you can't do anymore, there's a little thing called prayer. It may not change the situation, but it will change you in that situation. It will give you the strength to go on. It will give you the strength to move on. Prayer says to God, "I put my trust in You, Lord," for it is in you that we live, move, and have our being (Acts 17:28).

Live, my brother. Live, my sister.
Move, grow, and Live an abundant life.
LIVE.

Powerful Reflection & Application

1. Write down a time when you felt like giving up. How did you make it?

_____
_____
_____
_____
_____
_____
_____
_____
_____
_____
_____
_____
_____
_____
_____
_____
_____
_____
_____
_____

Thank God for getting you through that season and trust Him through whatever your next seasons bring.

2. Are you existing or living? Describe a time where you have been just existing.

3. How do you plan to intentionally live?

4. How will you know when you are living the abundant life?

5. What could be your anthem song (s) to fuel you with positivity and get you through the day?

_____
_____
_____
_____
_____
_____
_____
_____
_____
_____

This week, every morning when you awake, greet God in your own way. Buy a journal or notebook and record every positive moment you have within a day. If needed use some of the resources found in the back of this book or set up any medical appointments. Make it a point to take care of yourself and get some rest.

REMEMBER...
Power Point 1: LIVE
- ❖ God loves you.
- ❖ You are fearfully & wonderfully made on purpose for purpose.
- ❖ Choose to Live.
- ❖ Live intentionally in abundance and GROW.

Journal Entry

JOURNAL ENTRY

Pray

Proseuchomai (pros-yoo'-khom-ahee)

to pray to God, i.e., supplicate, worship

Chapter 2

Pray

God has blessed us with many gifts. The first gift, or Power Point He gave us, was the gift of life. This beautiful gift of life gave us the ability to love, spread peace, give joy and use the activity of our limbs to serve one another.

The next Power Point is the gift of prayer. Prayer, in my personal opinion, is one of the most powerful gifts. It can be viewed as a connector that positions us, protects, and provides. What is prayer to you? Do you see it as something powerful? How do you define prayer? Is it our norm to only shoot "arrow" or 911 prayers up in desperate or emotionally consuming situations? Is it something we only do in faith-based settings or church? Or is it something that only pastors, priests, and various ministers can effectively do?

Well, I hate to disappoint you, but prayer is not so deep and protected that God only hears ordained men and women of God. God hears the prayers of *all* of His children. The Bible tells us that the effectual, fervent prayer of the *righteous* (that is... *all* who are in right standing with God) avails much. Fervent prayer is heartfelt and a focused work. Therefore, we must understand that prayer is not meant to be our "genie in a bottle" or only our emergency 911 call to God.

Prayer is the foundation of our being and success. In the beginning, God gave us the gift of life and the gift of communication. God allowed us to speak, or communicate with Him, daily. That communication is called prayer. Prayer is not only a gift, but it is necessary to live the abundant life. Dr. Martin Luther King Jr. once said, "To be a Christian without prayer is no more possible than to be alive without breathing." Prayer is necessary, and it is a powerful gift that must be unwrapped and used daily if we are to live and not just merely exist.

Prayer was never meant to be a self-serving tool or a "drive-by" religious act, but a lifestyle. It is as important as the food you eat, the air you breathe, and the sleep your body needs to be healthy. Therefore, we must pray as if our very own life depends upon it. It is vital for our existence and for living life to the fullest.

PRAYER IS COMMUNICATION

Prayer is simply what it was created to be — communication. How can you get to know someone if you don't communicate with them regularly? Before a couple is married, they spend time together communicating with one another daily before they say, "I do," and become as one. Communication in a relationship is so important that one of the first things God did was have Adam name all of the animals and share those words with his wife, Eve. God wanted to ensure that there was communication among His creation and with Him. He made Himself available and accessible daily to build an intimate relationship with those He first created and for all future generations.

As we consider prayer in this vein, we must understand that there is authentic and general communication. Authentic communication is paramount in having a strong and successful relationship. It is different from the haphazard or general two-way communication of just exchanging information. It is an intentional, open, and honest way of sharing by both parties that results in a bond that cannot be broken. It requires more listening to the heart of the person and the content of what they are really saying. It is not interruptive, judgmental, or dismissive. It doesn't try to provide a quick solution that may not be a solution at all. Authentic communication can hear and see a person's heart and then provide insightful, honest, and meaningful recommendations for the person's benefit. In business relationships, it can bring mutually beneficial outcomes and profit. Therefore, this type of communication is vital for successful earthly relationships.

One could argue that authentic — intentional, open, honest, and loving communication is also necessary when praying to God. God wants to hear your heart.... your authentic self.... that fervent prayer. If we show up and pray authentically, the heart of God is fully accessed and responsive.

When we have a relationship with God, our hearts are open to Him and we are granted access to the Triune God. We have the Father whom we pray to and who responds with ultimate authority. We have the Son, Jesus Christ, our mediator in whose name we pray and how we are granted access to the throne of God. We also have the Holy Spirit who prays for us and in us! We have guaranteed access to our God, our Creator.

When Jesus died on the cross and shed His blood for our sin, the veil was torn in the Holy of Holies within the temple, symbolic of us having full access to the throne. We no longer had to go to an earthly priest who would take our sins to God in prayer. Jesus became our High Priest, our covering, our key, our reconciliatory entrance fee for communion, and uninhibited communication with God the Father.

Therefore, brethren, since we have confidence to enter the holy place by the blood of Jesus, by a new and living way which He inaugurated for us through the veil, that is, His flesh, and since we have a great priest over the house of God, let us draw near with a sincere heart in full assurance of faith, having our hearts sprinkled clean from an evil conscience and our bodies washed with pure water. (Hebrews 10:19-22 NKJV)

We pray to the Father through Jesus Christ, whose blood grants the believer access, and where the Holy Spirit hears the believer's heart and prays for them.

Likewise the Spirit also helps in our weaknesses. For we do not know what we should pray for as we ought, but the Spirit Himself makes intercession for us with groanings which cannot be uttered. Now He who searches the hearts knows what the mind of the Spirit is, because He makes intercession for the saints according to the will of God. (Romans 8:26-27 NKJV)

We must come into the knowledge and understanding that the Spirit of Truth, also known as the Holy Spirit, was provided for our daily benefit. He is our helper. In fact, the Spirit of Truth is a gift that we were given to communicate with and who will remain with us forever. Jesus tells us this in the Book of John, chapter 14:

> *"If you love Me, keep My commandments. And I will pray the Father, and He will give you another Helper, that He may abide with you forever— the **Spirit of Truth**, whom the world cannot receive, because it neither sees Him nor knows Him; but you know Him, for He dwells with you and will be in you. (John 14:15-17 NKJV)*

The Spirit of Truth speaks to us and guides us. He is our confidant, our counselor, and our personal intercessor. I like to think of Him as my best friend. He will teach you if you let him.

> *But the Helper, the Holy Spirit, whom the Father will send in My name, He will teach you all things, and bring to your remembrance all things that I said to you. (John 14:26 NKJV)*

There have been many times where I have said, "Something told me," or "Something inside of me wouldn't let me do or go…." Well, I realized for me that *Something* was the Spirit of Truth. He kept me from making some decisions that could have ended in dangerous outcomes. The Spirit of Truth, or the Holy Spirit (as we like to call Him) is not a mystic or ghost to be feared. He is a gift that Jesus asked God the Father to come and be our helper while we remain on earth. Isn't that beautiful? The Holy Spirit is assigned to each of us to communicate in and for us. So, we must position ourselves to actively and authentically listen to the Holy

Spirit. Then, do what we've heard (be obedient), and watch God move on our behalf.

God loves you and me. He wants that intimate, authentic relationship with us. Prayer is our lifeline. It connects us to our Creator, our Sustainer, and our Friend. He is our strength and our GPS system. Communicate — talk with, pray with your God.

As we understand communication from God's teaching, we should also consider the world's official definition. Communication, as defined by Miriam Webster, is to share, to transmit information, thought, or feeling so that it is satisfactorily received or understood. Prayer was given to us to commune with God. It is that gift that positions us to share, to transmit, to grow, and to build a closer relationship with God, our Creator. Prayer is a communication gift that was given to be desired, opened, and used authentically every day.

PURPOSE OF PRAYER: COMMUNE WITH GOD

In the beginning of human existence, it is recorded in the book of Genesis that Adam was communicating with God daily. Adam showed us that prayer is simply *sharing* your day with God. This is our first lesson on the purpose of prayer. In those first encounters with Adam, God demonstrated that prayer is more than communication, but includes a deeper concept of *communing* with Him. For prayer is not always about asking God for "things," telling God about our problems, or trying to manipulate a quick fix. As my husband, Pastor Rodric K. Reid would often say:

> *"Prayer was never created to be an aspirin, but a vitamin."*

God desires for us to daily commune with Him. In Jewish tradition, dinner was an intimate time when family came to "sup together." This was a time of sharing conversation and food. God wants us to "sup," to have supper — to share with Him.

God wants us to know from the beginning of creation that prayer is sharing our thoughts, our activities, and our desires with Him daily. It is being still and listening to His voice, His instruction. It is more than just talking. Prayer is intimate — an act of worship. To *commune* and share with God is a freeing experience.

If we would just invite God to *sup with* us, be His children, and share our day with God... what an amazing relationship we could develop with Him. As a little girl, before I would go to sleep, I would pray *with* the Lord. Meaning, I would commune and share with God about my day. I would tell him what took place, what I liked, and what I didn't like. Then, I would ask God to help me plan out my next day. What should I wear? Who should I talk to? What should I say? How was I going to help my mother? What or how should I help someone else? I would pause and wait to hear something back. Then, I would thank God for everything and everyone. That was my communication, my prayer, my communion time with God as a little child. The Bible tells us in Matthew 18:3:

"...Assuredly, I say to you, unless you are converted and become as little children, you will by no means enter the kingdom of heaven."

See yourself as God's child. Tell God everything about your day. Share with Him the good, the bad, and the ugly. Thank Him for listening. Thank God for being your friend. And even ask Him to help you plan your next day. And I promise you, you will have a peace that passes all understanding.

> *Rejoice always, **pray without ceasing**,*
> *and in everything give thanks, for this is the*
> *will of God. (1 Thessalonians 5:16-18 NKJV)*

Prayer can bring you hope, lift your countenance, and give you the strength to keep moving. I challenge you to share *everything* with God daily. Make an appointment with God. Put Him first on your calendar and keep the appointment like it's the most important appointment in the world. God has you on His calendar. So, don't keep canceling His appointment. Jesus demonstrated to us how important prayer is, as He made sure it was the first thing He did.

> *Now in the morning, having risen a long while before daylight,*
> *He went out and departed to a solitary place; and there He prayed.*
> *(Mark 1:35 NKJV)*

If Jesus communed with the Father daily, who are we to think that we don't need to? Before Jesus was crucified for us, He gave us another intimate, yet powerful, example through the last supper of how we can commune with Him. Partaking in this holy sacrament of receiving the elements of bread and wine representing the blessed body and blood of Jesus is another opportunity to speak and listen to the almighty God. It is an intimate time of healing, deliverance, and rejuvenation as it is a representative of our sin being washed away. Invite Jesus to *"sup"* with you, remembering that He shed His blood for you.

Maybe committing to praying and communing daily with God seems overwhelming. It seems like there is not enough time in the day. If you are not sure if you can commit or how to start intentionally setting aside time daily for God, pray this one prayer:

"God give me the desire to commune with you and help me make room for you." You can start with small steps. You may not have a prayer closet or an hour of time right now. So, start your communion time in the shower, in your car, in the laundry room, wherever you can *steal* away. In your own way, ask God to give you that desire that thirsts after Him. Pray that your thirst will be so great that you will not be satisfied, or your thirst quenched until after you have spent time with Him. God wants you to desire him. Desire Him and your life will change for the better. Thirst after God....

As the deer pants for streams of water,
so my soul pants for you, my God.
My soul thirsts for God, for the living God.
When can I go and meet with God. (Psalm 42:1-2 NIV)

Commune — share with God early and throughout your day. Share with God everything, including the secret things, thoughts, and feelings. Let your communication with Him be even better than when you shared those things with your best friend. Journal your prayers, your experiences, and your praises. Communion with God is more than a conversation between two, but a divine, intimate experience where unduplicated love and power is released for your good.

PURPOSE OF PRAYER: INCREASE OUR FAITH

God not only gave us prayer to communicate and commune with Him but as a gift that would teach us and increase our faith in this dark world.

Have you ever asked God for what seemed to be impossible? Has God ever worked out something better than you could have ever imagined? Has God ever come through for you just in the nick of time?

In any of those instances, your faith was increased. You know that because God helped you in the past, you can call on God to help you in your present and your future. God wanted to make sure we understood that faith — our belief and trust in Him — is what moves Him and pleases Him.

But without faith, it is impossible to please Him, for he who comes to God must believe that He is, and that He is a rewarder of those who diligently seek Him. (Hebrews 11:6 NKJV)

So, Jesus said to them, "... for assuredly, I say to you, if you have faith as a mustard seed, you will say to this mountain, 'Move from here to there,' and it will move; and nothing will be impossible for you. (Matthew 17:20 NKJV)

Prayer with faith unlocks closed doors. When you pray, pray to demonstrate that you have faith in God and His Word. Pray the Word of God for every situation. Pray the scriptures believing that Who you are praying to hears you and will answer.

Try filling in the blanks with your name in this prayer:

I_____ am more than a conqueror in Christ Jesus. I _____ am the head and Not the tail. When my enemies come to attack _____ they stumble and fall. For no weapon formed against _____ and my family shall prosper and every tongue that rises up against me I shall condemn. I _____ shall live and not die to proclaim the works of the Lord. Thank You, Lord, for loving me. Thank You for keeping me. I thank You, Lord, that your

grace abounds towards me and my family, and Your mercy is everlasting. Thank You for inclining Your ear unto me and hearing every petition. Thank You for being my Jehovah Rapha, the God that heals and restores; thank You for being my Jehovah Jireh, the God that provides. I love You forever and always.
In Jesus' name. Amen.

When you pray, you must believe that God is able to do exceedingly and abundantly above anything you could ask or think. If He has answered you or a family member before, He can do it again. Even if God does not move the way you desire Him to, it doesn't mean that He cannot. Part of our faith means we trust God with us, our children, our health, and whatever crisis or dream we may have. It is your faith, your trust, your *belief in action* that moves God and opens doors. God loves you and wants the best for you. Spend more time with Him, pray, build your faith and relationship with your Creator.

PRAYER IS A POWERFUL WEAPON
Ephesians 6:10-18 (NKJV)

*[10]Finally, my brethren, be strong in the Lord and in the power of His might. [11]Put on the whole armor of God, that you may be able to stand against the wiles of the devil. ... [17]And take the helmet of salvation, and the sword of the Spirit, which is the Word of God; [18]**praying always with all prayer and supplication in the Spirit,** being watchful to this end with all perseverance and supplication for all the saints—*

We are to pray at all times and about everything. Prayer is that *powerful* of a gift. Prayer is one of our weapons. After we have put on the whole armor of God standing strong in the faith, we need to seal it with prayer. Praying always with all prayer means: in public, private, mentally, verbally in front of family members, in school, or in a restaurant. Pray in *All* your different ways.

Not only does the scripture say we are to pray, but we are also to pray with supplication. The first part of prayer in this context actually means to pray for the blessings. In that second part, the word supplication in its original meaning is to pray against evil, to avert evil, and to war in the Spirit. It points out that we are not to be so concerned about ourselves as we stand there suited up, but we are also to pray with all supplication for the saints. *Why?* Because we wrestle not against flesh and blood, but against evil.

Therefore, in the name of Jesus the Christ, the Son of the living God, because of His blood that was shed on the Cross and the resurrection power, Jesus has now all authority. Because you are God's child — an heir — you can take authority over all evil, praying in the Spirit with all supplication. You can cast down strongholds and plead the blood of Jesus over you, your family, and your communities.

Take now thy authority. Put on the whole armor of God daily and pray in faith the Word of God with all prayer and supplication. Prayer is a weapon. It protects, defends, and covers. Prayer is a powerful gift. It connects, positions, and protects us. Prayer is intimate and powerful. It is a blessing, and one of our greatest weapons.

LORD TEACH US TO PRAY

God really wanted us to understand the importance of prayer, so He had it recorded in His scripture that even Jesus will be praying for us on our behalf. I can't think of anyone else I would want praying for me, can you? The disciples recognized that the prayers of Jesus brought results. They recognized the power of prayer and asked Jesus, "Lord teach us how to pray." The disciples knew that He had a direct line to the Father. They had watched Him. They saw Him go in weak and come out strong. They watched Him pray over food that was meant for one person and feed over 5000. They asked, *"Lord teach me how to pray."* They saw Him pray to the Father and eyesight be restored. *"Lord teach me how to pray!"* They saw Him praying to the Father for the dead to be resurrected. Lazarus come forth! *"Lord teach us how to pray!"* We've seen the Pharisees and Sadducees. We prayed ourselves. But we've never seen mountains move because of our prayers. We've never seen the blind healed or the sick restored from our prayers. *"Lord teach us how to pray!"* He taught them what we now call the Lord's Prayer:

Our Father which art in heaven, Hallowed be Thy name; Thy kingdom come, Thy will be done on earth as it is in heaven. Give us this day our daily bread and forgive us our trespasses as we forgive those who trespass against us. Lead us not into temptation but deliver us from evil. For Thine is the kingdom, the power and the glory forever, Amen. (Matthew 6:9-13)

We not only need to learn methods on prayer, but we also need the motivation to pray. So, Lord Teach Us to PRAY. There have been times when I didn't want to pray, and I'm sure you have had some of those times too. Let's pray together:

Lord, teach US to Pray. Teach us that there is power in our voice, and all we need to do is open up our mouths and cry out. We do not need a lot of words, only a sincere heart. Lord, give us the desire to seek you daily. Teach us to pray in the bad as well as the good times. In your name, we pray, Amen.

God is our Father. A Father that is like no other. His love for us is pure and strong. He is positioned high above us and holy. He is a King above any king or kingdom here on earth. He has the only true power to feed and provide both physically and spiritually. God, our Father, has the only true power to forgive and deliver us from evil. He does all of this because He loves us. God wants us to grow in Him, and in our communication with Him. God wants to bless us, provide and protect us. But most importantly, God just wants to commune with us. We were created to commune with Him, to share everything with Him. Prayer is a powerful gift. Let us open it up and use this unique, powerful gift that keeps on giving. Open this gift of prayer daily and be blessed beyond measure. I challenge you — Ask God today:

"Lord teach me how to pray."

Powerful Reflection & Application

1. Put God on your calendar and authentically share with Him. Pray to God now and tell Him about your day. Write down your experience. What did you share with God?

_____
_____
_____
_____
_____
_____
_____
_____
_____
_____
_____
_____
_____
_____
_____
_____
_____
_____
_____
_____
_____
_____

2. What prayers have God answered for you? How has your faith increased?

PRAY

3. How will you make prayer your daily vitamin?

_____
_____
_____
_____
_____
_____
_____
_____
_____
_____
_____
_____
_____
_____
_____

4. Find Bible scriptures that you can put your name or your family's name in as you pray. Write down at least one.

_____
_____
_____
_____
_____
_____
_____
_____

5. Describe a time when the Holy Spirit spoke to you.

This week schedule your daily appointments with God. Identify a special place in your home, for just you and God to talk. Ask Him to join you over a cup of coffee, tea, or water. Take your notebook or journal to record your prayers and God's words. Keep your daily appointments with God and enjoy your peaceful time with Him.

REMEMBER...
Power Point 2: Pray
- ❖ God gave us the gift of life and communication.
- ❖ God loves us and he created us to commune/share with Him and creation.
- ❖ Pray authentically daily, as it is our daily vitamin.
- ❖ Prayer is one of the most powerful gifts from God.

JOURNAL ENTRY

Journal Entry

Aphiēmi (af-ee'-ay-mee)

to let go, give up a debt, forgive, to remit

Chapter 3

Forgive

    Power point number three is to forgive. Forgiveness can save your life. Forgiveness is health to the soul and body. So, why is it so hard for us to forgive? Some people like to hold grudges, but when you hold in all that bitterness and all that anger, you're only harming yourself. It's not good for your body, mind, or soul. Someone once said,

> *"Unforgiveness is choosing to stay trapped in a jail cell of bitterness, serving time for someone else's crime."* ~Anonymous

    When I was in sports, I was very competitive. I played basketball and ran track. Whatever I competed in, I wanted to win. Who wants or likes to lose, right? I like winning outside of sports too. In my younger days, I applied that same competitive nature to forgiveness. If we get upset with someone and hold onto that bitterness, anger, or resentment, we have lost. Nine times out of ten, they have moved on, living life, climbing the career ladder, or happy with someone else and not thinking about us. They are happy and free. Yet, we are bitter and in bondage. We are the ones serving jail time, not them. We have lost. We are the only ones on the basketball team, at work, at home, in the classroom with an attitude, a headache, or experiencing extreme anxiety when we see those who we've not forgiven. Unlike us, they have moved on. Bishop T.D. Jakes speaks to the importance of forgiveness in *Let it Go*, when he says, "Unforgiveness is like drinking poison and waiting for the other person to die."

We are waiting for them to suffer or die when we are the ones suffering and dying inside. Again, in most cases, the person who has done something wrong against you, after a certain amount of time, is no longer thinking about you. When unforgiveness in my life revolved around a relationship, I realized that person had moved on with someone else and was not thinking about me. So, why was I still holding on? I pose the same question to you. Why are you still holding on to stuff? Why are we allowing ourselves to be miserable; not sleeping at night, overeating, or participating in self-sabotage? We're losing when we need to WIN.

FORGIVE FOR THE HEALTH OF IT

We can't allow unforgiveness, nor the offspring of unforgiveness — bitterness and resentment to take root in us. If we do, that poison will slowly attack our spirit, soul, and body, killing us softly. We need to forgive for the health of it.

Loren Toussaint, Ph.D., a professor of psychology at Luther College in Decorah, Iowa, said that forgiveness is "the true mind-body connection." According to many studies, forgiveness plays a role in both our mental and physical health. The Mayo Clinic states that those who forgive have:

- Healthier relationships
- Improved mental health
- Less anxiety, stress, and hostility
- Lower blood pressure
- Fewer symptoms of depression
- A stronger immune system
- Improved heart health
- Improved self-esteem

Therefore, the benefits of forgiving are primarily for us, not just the offender. When we forgive, we win. When we forgive, the coping mechanisms of self-sabotage: drugs, tobacco, alcohol, cutting, sex, etc., are no longer needed. When we forgive, the poison dissipates, and we are able to rest. Our anxiety lessens and our heart feels and works better. We are no longer sleeping our life away, and bitterness no longer consumes us. We are no longer stuck in time deeply depressed, but we are moving up out of that dark place, rediscovering our purpose, and becoming emotionally able to experience peace and joy.

Forgive, for your body and mind desires and needs to be healthy. Don't let unforgiveness win. Choose to forgive, let go, and be released from the bondage. You've been in the jail of unforgiveness long enough. Your mind and body have suffered long enough. It may not be easy, but it is necessary. Jesus wants you to be emotionally free. Choose today to forgive for the health of it.

WHAT IS FORGIVENESS?

One day, I realized that I had been miserable long enough. I decided, in the spirit of competition, that I couldn't let my perpetrators, my enemies, my abusers, nor my naysayers, win. I had to let go. I had to forgive. I wanted to live the abundant life. I wanted to be healthy mentally, physically, and spiritually. I wanted to forgive "for the health of it." However, I realized that I did not know what true forgiveness was or how to achieve it.

Viewing forgiveness solely in the vein of competition was the type of thinking before I knew God. However, there is more to forgiveness than mere competitive thinking. God doesn't want us to live in unforgiveness.

So, what is forgiveness? Well, I looked it up in Webster's Dictionary. Forgiveness is defined as:

> *to grant pardon (release) for an offense, a debt; to grant pardon to a person; to give up all claim on an account; to cease to feel resentment, and to cancel the indebtedness or liability of.*

Simply put, forgiveness is releasing control of the offense and its emotional bondage (i.e., resentment, bitterness) in your life. To break it down even further, the word forgive can be divided into two words — *for* and *give*. It is something we give to others before they have an opportunity to even ask to be forgiven. It is a gift that we get the strength to do with God's help. It is a gift that releases both the offender and the offended. When we gain the strength to forgive, to pardon even when the person doesn't deserve it, and when we are not expecting anything in return, it is a gift that blesses us and our offender.

Webster's definition is good and useful. It indirectly addresses the mind. We have already discussed the importance and value of forgiveness for our body, but what about our spirit? What does God say about forgiveness? The book of Ephesians, chapter 4 verses 31 through 32 (NET) states:

> *You must put away all bitterness, anger, wrath, quarreling, and slanderous talk—indeed all malice. Instead, be kind to one another, compassionate, forgiving one another, just as God in Christ also forgave you.*

Our forgiveness is to mirror Divine forgiveness. It tells us in Mathew 6:14-15 (NKJV):

> *For if you forgive men their trespasses, your heavenly Father will also forgive you. But if you do not forgive men their trespasses, neither will your Father forgive your trespasses.*

God forgave us before we even knew who we were. God made a way of escape through His Son, Jesus, so we can be reconciled back to God the Father. God loved us so much that He gave us (He sacrificed) His Son so we could spend an eternity with Him (Jn 3:16). Therefore, Divine forgiveness was made possible through the sacrifice and shedding of the blood. Jesus Christ was our Passover lamb, our sacrifice that shed His blood for our wrongdoings, for our sin.

> *And according to the Law, ... all things are cleansed with blood, and without shedding of blood there is no forgiveness. (Hebrews 9:22 NASB)*

God loves you and me so much. He wants us to have life AND life more abundantly. God wants to spend eternity with you. God in His infinite wisdom knew that we were going to make mistakes, do some things, and say some things that were not pleasing to people, and definitely not pleasing to Him. He knew that we would sin against Him. He knew that we would be unforgiving, but thank God for His grace and mercy! Thank God, He had a way of escape, a "key" for our sin! So, we wouldn't forget, God had this "key" that could unlock the chains to release us from our own prison written down:

> *If you confess your sins, He is faithful and righteous to forgive us our sins and to cleanse us from all unrighteousness. (1 John 1:9 NKJV)*

Confession is the "key." Confessing is simply to acknowledge, to admit, to tell God you've done wrong. When we use the key of confession, it is our heart that turns the key and unlocks the prison doors. When we confess our sin and our wrongdoings with a contrite heart, God throws our sins into a sea of forgetfulness. There is nothing that you have done that God doesn't know about. Talk to God and be real with Him. Be transparent and pour out to Him. Confess with a sincere heart and tell Him you're sorry and ask for His forgiveness. There is nothing you've done that is so bad that He will not forgive. He forgives ALL sin.

> *I acknowledged my sin to You,*
> *And I did not hide my guilt;*
> *I said, "I will confess my wrongdoings to the Lord";*
> *And You forgave the guilt of my sin. (Psalm 32:5 NASB)*

FORGIVE YOURSELF

Sometimes forgiveness is hard because we are the person who needs to be forgiven. Maybe we did something that society considers horrible. Whatever *that* horrible thing is, we want to keep it to ourselves or believe there is no way God would forgive us for "that." Maybe we had an abortion, did drugs, cheated, were the abuser, or the one who pulled the trigger. Whatever "that" may be, God forgives you. The Bible says that God is faithful and just to forgive you of <u>all</u> of your sins. It is not some of your debts or some of your wrongdoings. He does not just forgive the lies told, but He also forgives the lives that may have been taken. It is not just the little bitty sin, but ALL of your sin. Sin is sin. Wrongdoing is just wrong, and God forgives it all.

God also tells us in the Bible, He forgives us as far as the east is to the west. The east and west never meet. Therefore, God's forgiveness is forever!

So, why can't you forgive yourself?

Once you have asked God to forgive you and He honors His promise and does it, you too must forgive yourself. You must pardon and release yourself from the guilt and shame. You cannot continue to crawl around in self-hatred, pity, guilt, or shame. You have to be transformed like the caterpillar that sheds off skin layers of self-sabotage, guilt, and shame, and then transforms into a beautiful butterfly. No matter what you've done, you can acknowledge what you've done, understand why it happened, and choose to know that you are NOT defined by what you have done. You and I are not perfect, and we have made small and large mistakes. Pray and ask God to help you forgive yourself and to release yourself from the bondage of blame, shame, and guilt.

Understand that in forgiving ourselves emotionally, we are accepting our responsibility in the wrongdoing, but letting go of the self-punishment. Some of us have punished ourselves long enough. It's time to pardon ourselves. God forgave us. Therefore, we must forgive, let go, and release ourselves understanding that we are imperfect, yet valuable. Say that out loud, "I am imperfect, yet valuable." God sees you and me in all of our faults and still loves us. God still has purpose inside of us. We are valuable in our imperfection. God doesn't make any junk. When He made us, He said we were good. Therefore, there is good in us. We are not what we did. We are not our own offense. We are not failures.

Get up from crawling like a caterpillar (if that is you), and forgive yourself. How? I'm not sure how or what that looks like for you. I am not an expert, nor do I claim to have all the answers. Everyone is different and uniquely created by God. What I can do is share some tips that helped me to self-forgive.

- o Prayer was and is my first line of recovery.
- o Journaling through written form and with voice apps all of my thoughts, but making sure they included something positive.
- o Having positive affirmations and values written in places that were visible to me and not so much to others.
- o Intentionally putting into practice the positive values that I wanted to see in myself.
- o Practicing self-love. I had done enough self-sabotaging.
- o Getting Understanding.
    - ✓ Understand that God really loves me.
    - ✓ Understand that I cannot change the past, but I can change my way of thinking and change my future.

- ✓ Understand that I can help others by sharing how I overcame the same "wrongdoings" and experiences.
- ✓ Understand that I can forgive myself and be released to fully enjoy God's peace.

Remember, God, forgives you. If you need to pray, to confess one more time, to believe the truth that God can and will forgive you, let Psalm 51:1-2, 8-14 (NLT) be your prayer today:

> *[1] "Purify me from my sins, and I will be clean;*
> *[2] wash me, and I will be whiter than snow.*
> *[8] Oh, give me back my joy again;*
> *you have broken me—*
> *Now let me rejoice.*
> *[9] Don't keep looking at my sins.*
> *Remove the stain of my guilt.*
> *[10] Create in me a clean heart, O God.*
> *Renew a loyal spirit within me.*
> *[11] Do not banish me from your presence,*
> *and don't take your Holy Spirit from me.*
> *[12] Restore to me the joy of your salvation,*
> *and make me willing to obey you.*
> *[13] Then I will teach your ways to rebels,*
> *and they will return to you.*
> *[14] Forgive me for shedding blood, O God who saves;*
> *then I will joyfully sing of your forgiveness.*

God, I confess my sin of _____, and all of my wrongdoings. Thank you for listening and hearing my heart in this confession. God, I receive the promise of Your forgiveness. Now, help me in this journey to forgive myself. Help me, Spirit of Truth.

Show me the way. Help me to forgive myself. Remove shame and guilt. I have confessed my sin, my shame, and my guilt to You. So now, I confess my victory — "I forgive me." Let these words of victory take up residence in me. What I did will no longer have control over me and my thinking. In Jesus's, name I pray and stand on your Word. Thank you, God, Amen.

Let this be the day that you start the journey of forgiving yourself. If you can't do it on your own, seek counseling. God placed gifts inside of others to be His counselors here on earth. It might take a few attempts to find a counselor who is the best fit for you. Don't give up. Keep praying, keep pressing, and practice self-love until self-forgiveness is evident because God loves us and sees our value. God wants us to live life and life more abundantly.

FORGIVENESS IS A PROCESS

Just like God forgives us for everything, God wants us to not only forgive ourselves but to forgive one another.

*"...bearing with one another, and forgiving one another, if anyone has a complaint against another; even as Christ forgave you, so you also **must** do. (Colossians 3:13 NKJV)*

In most cases, forgiving others is easier said than done. Just as it was a sacrifice that granted us Divine forgiveness, it is also going to take us sacrificing some things like our pride, stubbornness, and emotions to forgive others. In addition to sacrifice, if we are to mirror Divine forgiveness, for some of us, like it was for Christ, forgiveness may be painful to do. It might cause others to talk about us or even give us backlash for forgiving a guilty person who did us wrong. However, remember that Jesus sacrificed and experienced pain beyond comprehension. He was beaten and talked about for our Divine forgiveness. Christ sacrificed Himself to give us another opportunity to get right with God. Therefore, we, too, must forgive sacrificially and sometimes go through pain so that we can regain our rightful positions, like Christ, with God the Father.

We need to understand that forgiveness is a process. It is a process of the mind that manifests action and releases peace and power. Jesus went through a process. While in the Garden of Gethsemane, Jesus sweated tears of blood as He prayed and thought about what He was getting ready to go through and sacrifice for our forgiveness (Luke 22:44). Through a process in His mind, He was truly moved by faith to "not my will, but your (God, the Father's) will be done." Through a process, Jesus was charged, unjustly imprisoned, ridiculed, beaten, carried the cross (burden), endured pain, shed blood, encouraged others, interceded for the unjust. Even in the midst of His pain, He prayed forgiveness for His perpetrators. WOW! Once Jesus released them, "Father forgive them for they know not what they do" (Luke 23:34), and through the finished work of forgiveness for the world, His blood filled the streets, and Jesus was released to His rightful position with all power. Again, forgiveness is a process of the mind that manifests action and releases peace and power.

Some horrible things may have happened to you or someone you know. Those things are deeper than just forgiving a person who stepped on your foot or called you out of your birth name. Those deeper situations (i.e., molestation, rape, loved one murdered, infidelity, child abuse, etc.) can make it emotionally difficult to forgive.

But God isn't asking us to do anything that He didn't do Himself. It was emotionally difficult to say, *"Not my will God, but*

Yours," and to forgive us not with just His mind and heart, but with His body and life. Not to mention that while Jesus went through His process, He had people lie on Him, talk about Him, and abuse Him physically and mentally. They disrespected Him, betrayed Him, murdered His family members, jailed Him unjustly, and so much more.

Forgiveness may not be easy, but it is necessary.

This is why God's Word tells us to forgive. God truly understands the arduous process we have to experience, but that process should lead us to the ultimate self-sacrificing act of forgiveness that manifests peace, and power. Understand that while we are in the process, we may experience shock, isolation, anger, grief, or depression. Yet, we cannot stay there. Jesus was down in the Garden of Gethsemane, but He got up. He didn't stay there. Jesus was down three days after the cross, and then He rose. He GOT UP! After a while, we must get up too. We can't stay crawling on the ground. We have to choose to go through the process of forgiveness so we can experience the transformation of the butterfly and be released with peace and new positions of power. How do you get up, one might ask? How can you rise from the pain, embarrassment, unexplainable hurt, or bitterness to forgive?

1. Remember, God is your help in EVERY need.
2. Ask God to Help. *Casting all your cares upon Him, for He cares for you.* (1 Peter 5:7 NKJV) Acknowledge what has happened, and allow yourself to go through the grieving process.

However, one has to ask God for help because we cannot do this on our own.

3. Release it — Give it all to God. Jesus released the perpetrators (which includes us), and He released Himself to God the Father (Luke 23:46). Therefore, you and I must release unforgiveness and any additional sin it brings to our spirit, soul, and body. Give it to God. Give every care, including anger towards God, every disappointment, anxiety, and hurt, to God. *Come unto me, all you who labor and are heavy laden... for my yoke is easy and my burden is light.* (Matthew 11:28-30)

4. Trust God to lift you. *Trust in the Lord with all your heart, and lean not on your own understanding. In all your ways acknowledge Him, and He shall direct your paths.* (Proverbs 3:5 NKJV) You and I may not understand how we will get through the process, how the depression will be lifted, how the weeping can cease, or how the nightmares can end, but trust GOD anyway. Every day, acknowledge Him and His goodness despite the circumstances. Every day, praise Him for delivering you and healing you through the process, even though you cannot see or feel it. Trust God through the process. Again, together you can rise. Just as God raised Jesus, He can raise you. He can raise you *NOT* as a god, but raise you out and up from the grave of sin and unforgiveness. After you get up, trust God to direct your paths. Those paths may include a therapist and that is okay. Those paths may include helping the very one who hurt you and that's okay. However, without question, those paths will lead you to righteousness (right standing with God), and new positions of freedom (peace) and power.

How Many Times Do We Forgive?

Again, forgiveness requires us to pardon — to release others from the penalty. Pardon speaks to the smallest, as well to the deepest of offenses towards us. When Jesus pardoned us, when He shed His blood for us, He released us from the penalty of our sin. He released us from eternal death. Jesus demonstrated His love for us; so, we must demonstrate our love for Him and His finished work by releasing others.

We must understand that we are to forgive even when the offender doesn't deserve it. Our act of forgiveness is not dependent upon what the person has done. Forgiveness does not come in degrees, nor does it have clauses. The onus — the responsibility is on us to forgive. Forgiveness is about what we do. Forgiveness *frees and releases us*.

When we pardon our enemies — those who have done us wrong — not only are we releasing them, but we also experience release from hatred, bitterness, pain, or bondage of various kinds. Jesus' sacrifice and death on the cross paid the penalty for the many wrongdoings we would commit. Remember, God forgave us when we didn't deserve it; we kept on sinning, over and over. He forgave us when we kept being disobedient to Him and His Word. He forgave us when we didn't love our neighbor as ourselves; when we hurt others, and ourselves, and when we rejected Him. He forgave and still forgives us. Jesus' sacrifice and death on the cross for us opened a door of unlimited forgiveness.

Jesus explained it to Peter like this:

> *Then Peter came to Him and said, 'Lord, how often shall my brother sin against me, and I forgive him? Up to seven times?' Jesus said to him, 'I do not say to you, up to seven times, but up to seventy times seven.' (Matthew 18:21-22 NKJV)*

Seventy times seven does not literally equal 490 times in this example. There is not a "forgiveness cap" with loopholes or exceptions. Jesus does not cap us off, only forgiving us 490 times, nor only forgiving certain offenses. Aren't you grateful that you have more than 490 chances? Some of us used all of those up before high school. I thank and praise God that my forgiveness is not based on my offense, but on what God has already done! I thank and praise God that His love for me is greater, and He did not put a "forgiveness cap" on my life.

Since seventy times seven is not about math, Jesus is telling Peter and us to forgive EVERY time.

Every time an offensive act is committed against us, we are to focus on forgiving. Every time a trigger or a remembrance of the offense comes to mind, we have to cast it down and replace it with an affirmation and an attitude of forgiveness.

Every time someone does you wrong, in your Spirit, do what Jesus did — He prayed. Pray, "Father forgive them — I forgive them for they know not what they do." Pray for your enemies. Pray and ask God to help you forgive. Pray for your thinking to be transformed. Pray for your own deliverance from unforgiveness and bitterness.

If Jesus got on that cross, hung high, and let people spit on Him, talk about Him, stab Him, all for you and me; if He did all of that so He can forgive you, and me, then why can't we forgive others?

As you look at the cross that Jesus had to bear, think about what He's done for you on that cross. Think about all the beatings He took and all the blood and water that came out of His body just to forgive us (wow). He said if I did that for you — if I laid down my life for you, then why can't you forgive your brother who just cussed you out? Why can't you forgive your sister who tried to take your man? Why can't you forgive the person who lied to you and got you fired? Why can't you forgive the drunk driver? Why can't you forgive the one who took something precious from you?

Jesus is our example.

> *He did not retaliate when he was insulted, nor threaten revenge when he suffered. He left his case in the hands of God, who always judges fairly. (1 Peter 2:23 NLT)*

Jesus taught us not to cast a stone at someone else's wrongdoings when we have done wrong ourselves.

He also demonstrated forgiveness when He forgave Judas who betrayed Him. Judas was the disciple who turned Jesus in to the authorities for money and treated Him like He was property. Jesus forgave those who killed His cousin, John the Baptist. He forgave His friend, Peter, who denied knowing Him and turned his back on Him. Jesus forgave those who lied on Him. He forgave those who talked about Him and spat on Him. Jesus forgave those who beat Him and stabbed Him. He forgave those who made Him bleed. He forgave those responsible for killing Him, which includes you and I. Remember, in His own words He called out to God, *"Father forgive them, for they know not what they do."* (Luke 23:34 KJV)

Forgiveness is not easy, but it is necessary. Jesus' example to us demonstrates obedience, humility, and sacrifice. Again, agreeing to go through that sacrificial process may not make sense. After all, one might think, "They don't deserve my forgiveness. They were wrong. They broke the law. They hurt me. They took something or someone from me." You're right. They may deserve the punishment for the offense, but that punishment is for God to hand down. We cannot allow unforgiveness to consume us, control our lives, and steal our joy. Forgiveness is our responsibility to God, and ourselves. Forgiveness is for us to be released from the emotional pain so we can win. Forgiveness is necessary so that we can be healthy and live life and life more abundantly. Forgiveness is necessary so we can be repositioned into a place of peace and power.

Powerful Reflection & Application

1. Is there anyone you need to forgive?

It can be someone from childhood, a co-worker, a stranger, a friend, associate, family member, or someone else. Think about it. If there are people you have thought of, write their names below and ask God to help you to forgive them.

_____
_____
_____
_____
_____
_____
_____
_____
_____
_____
_____
_____
_____
_____
_____
_____
_____
_____
_____
_____

2. You are valuable to God. Take a moment and confess in prayer any wrongdoings that you have committed in your past or present. You can also write them down below if you want.

___

3. Is there anything you need to forgive yourself for? Dig deep within yourself and be honest. If there is anything, write it down below.

4. What are some of the steps you're going to take to move past the pain and the hurt of unforgiveness?

_____
_____
_____
_____
_____
_____
_____
_____
_____
_____
_____

5. Thank God for reminding you about the importance of forgiveness. Thank God for helping you in this area of forgiveness. Thank God for His forgiveness.

_____
_____
_____
_____
_____
_____
_____
_____

This week if you have unforgiveness for someone write a letter to them in your journal. Take time to breathe, move forward and love on you.

REMEMBER...
Power Point 3: Forgive
- ❖ God forgives You.
- ❖ Forgive for the Health of It.
- ❖ Forgive Yourself. You are not what you've done.
- ❖ Forgiveness is not easy, but it is necessary.
- ❖ God forgave you and we are to mirror His Divine forgiveness to others.
- ❖ Forgiveness is a process, and it releases us into our rightful positions of peace and power.
- ❖ Forgive so that you can live the abundant life.
- ❖ God Loves You.

JOURNAL ENTRY

Journal Entry

SUMMARY

With all sincerity, thank you for reading *Power Points 4 Living: Practical Applications for a Successful Life*. I challenge you to take the information from this book and apply it to your daily walk with God. The worst thing you can do is let this book sit on a shelf, like other books, where it will have no impact. Remember, you were created by God. You are a valuable gift. You were created on purpose for a purpose. Therefore, choose to live and not exist. Choose to live the abundant life. Discover your anthem song and G.R.O.W. Make an appointment with God every day and keep it. Use your voice, for it is powerful. You need to be intentional and pray (talk to God about everything daily). Let go of those things that keep you from living the abundant life. Let go of fear and unforgiveness. Forgive for the health of it. Forgive because God forgave you and He wants you to be free, experiencing life like a butterfly — higher up from lower ground.

It is my greatest hope that *Power Points 4 Living: Practical Applications for a Successful Life* has blessed you in some way. It is my prayer that this book has challenged you to know yourself, your community, and your God in a deeper and more significant way so that you may successfully walk out your destiny and live the abundant life.

Now to Him who is able to do exceedingly abundantly above all that we ask or think, according to the power that works in us, to Him be glory in the church by Christ Jesus to all generations, forever and ever. Amen. (Ephesians 3:20-21 NKJV)

Live in Power!

CURRENT RESOURCES

ONLINE BIBLE
https://www.biblegateway.com/

STOP SMOKING / STOP VAPING (JUULING/DABBING)
1-800-784-8669 (Quit NOW)www.Smokefree.gov
www.truthinitiative.org

ADDICTION SERVICES
SAMHSA National Helpline:1-800-662-4357
https://www.samhsa.gov/

NATIONAL ALLIANCE ON MENTAL ILLNESS (NAMI)
1-800-950-NAMI (6264) Monday through Friday, 10 am–8 pm, EST
Text: NAMI to 741741 for 24/7 confidential free crisis counseling
www.nami.org

LIFE COACHING
Power Points 4 Living, L.L.C.
www.powerpoints4living.com
info@powerpoints4living.com

DUO EMPOWERMENT SERVICES
https://duogiggles.weebly.com/

YOUR LOCAL CHURCH

NATIONAL DOMESTIC VIOLENCE HOTLINE
1-800-799-7233(SAFE)
www.ndvh.org

NATIONAL HUMAN TRAFFICKING RESOURCE CENTER
1-800-373-7888
Text: HELP to 233733 (BeFree)
www.polarisproject.org

NATIONAL SUICIDE PREVENTION LIFELINE
1-800-273-8255 (TALK) Available 24 hours
www.suicidepreventionlifeline.org

SMALL BUSINESS ADMINISTRATION
www.sba.gov

ABOUT THE AUTHOR

Tisha Reid is passionate about helping people maximize their strengths and operate within their purpose. She is recognized as a women's health advocate, community mobilizer, and anointed preacher of the Gospel. She has impacted many lives through life-changing workshops, coaching, health programming, and powerful preaching.

A native of Indianapolis, Tisha is a graduate of Cathedral High and holds a Bachelor of Science in Public Health from Indiana University. She received her license to preach in 1999 and was ordained in 2004 in Christian Ministry. Currently, Tisha serves as Associate Pastor at Mt. Vernon Ave. AME Church in Columbus, Ohio, where her husband, Rodric K. Reid is the Senior Pastor.

To her professional credit, Tisha has developed community health programming addressing health equity for over 20 years. Currently, she is the Director of Health Equity & Cancer Control for the Indiana Clinical Translational Sciences Institute's, Connections IN Health, in Indianapolis, IN. She serves on numerous statewide boards and is a member of Alpha Kappa Alpha Sorority, Inc, serving in the Alpha Sigma Omega Chapter in Columbus Ohio.

Tisha is an entrepreneur providing organizational training and certified life coaching for individuals and organizations. You can attend her monthly Power Points 4 Living webinars or follow her on social media through her business PowerPoints4Living. She is available for speaking engagements, workshops, and book clubs. Please contact her at info@powerpoints4living.com to learn more about her business or book her for your empowerment (coaching, speaking engagements, workshop) needs.

Family is very important to Tisha. As a loving wife and mother, she enjoys spending time with her husband and their three gifted daughters: Jasmin, Tiffani, and Jessica. Tisha Reid is simply a child of God serving the community so she can hear God say, *"Well done My good and faithful servant, well done."*

Tisha Reid, CEO
Power Points 4 Living, L.L.C.

FOR MORE INFORMATION:
www.powerpoints4living.com
info@powerpoints4living.com
Follow us on Facebook

Made in USA
Columbus, OH
12 April 2021

$20.00
ISBN 978-0-578-87357-2
52000>

www.ingramcontent.com/pod-product-compliance
Lightning Source LLC
Chambersburg PA
CBHW050655160426
43194CB00010B/1942